CODING
with
THE PARANORMAL

BY KYLIE BURNS

Express!

BELLWETHER MEDIA • MINNEAPOLIS, MN

Imagination comes alive in Express! Transform the everyday into the fresh and new, discover ways to stir up flavor and excitement, and experiment with new ideas and materials. Express! makerspace books: where your next creative adventure begins!

This edition first published in 2024 by Bellwether Media, Inc.

No part of this publication may be reproduced in whole or in part without written permission of the publisher. For information regarding permission, write to Bellwether Media, Inc., Attention: Permissions Department, 6012 Blue Circle Drive, Minnetonka, MN 55343.

Library of Congress Cataloging-in-Publication Data

LC record for Coding with the Paranormal available at: https://lccn.loc.gov/2023022004

Text copyright © 2024 by Bellwether Media, Inc. EXPRESS and associated logos are trademarks and/or registered trademarks of Bellwether Media, Inc.

Editors: Sarah Eason and Christina Leaf
Illustrator: Eric Smith
Series Design: Brittany McIntosh
Graphic Designer: Paul Myerscough

Printed in the United States of America, North Mankato, MN.

TABLE OF CONTENTS _ □ X

Coding is the way humans **communicate** instructions to computers. Computers need us to tell them what to do. But we must communicate that in a way computers can understand. **Code** is a tool that programmers, or coders, use to give **commands** to a computer.

Coding is fun, and anyone can learn how to do it!

Unplugged coding is coding without a computer! It involves activities that build coding skills such as problem-solving and **decomposition**, just like coding with a computer. The unplugged activities in this book help develop skills that take the mystery out of coding. For extra fun, we will use the **paranormal** as our theme!

LET'S GET STARTED!

One of the most important skills in coding is problem-solving. A programmer solves problems by first understanding what needs to be done and then creating a list of steps for actions. Then they turn the steps into code so the computer can follow them to complete the task correctly.

- a timer
- a package of dry spaghetti
- a package of mini marshmallows
- a flat, sturdy surface for building

In this problem-solving activity, you and a friend were assigned a mission for the government. You must build towers to watch for **UFOs** using only dry spaghetti and mini marshmallows! See who can build the tallest tower to more easily see otherworldly visitors!

LET'S GET STARTED!

1

Choose a flat surface, such as the floor or a tabletop, to work on.

6

2

Set out half of the dry spaghetti and the mini marshmallows for each person so they are easy to reach.

3

Set the timer for 5 minutes.

4

Start the timer and start building your tower!

5

When the timer ends, stop building.

6

Compare the heights of your towers. The person with the tallest tower wins!

TURN THE PAGE TO SEE HOW YOU DID!

DID YOU KNOW?

Some researchers have developed codes to reach out to aliens in outer space. They have sent one code into space, but so far no replies have been received!

How tall were you able to build your UFO watchtower? Did it look like the one below? Did you come across problems? What did you do to solve them? How do you think the mission would have turned out if you used large marshmallows instead?

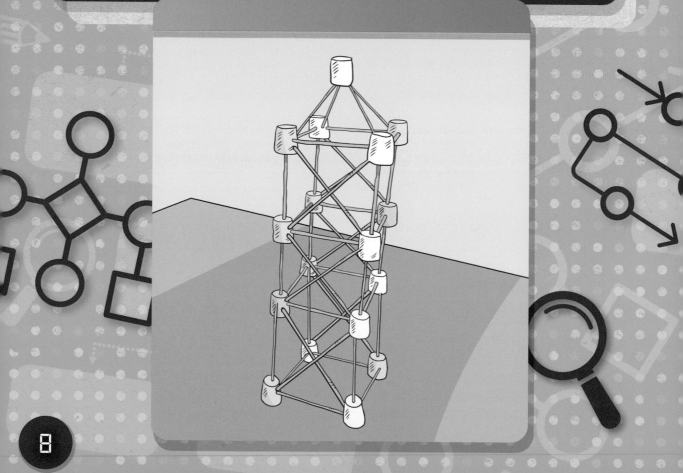

Coders want to write the best, fastest program they can. When you solve problems, do not just think about how to prevent or fix something. Instead, ask yourself if you can do something that would improve your idea.

CODING CHALLENGE! ⎵ ☐ X

Try the same activity a few more times. Change how you solve the problem by adding one, or all, of the following. How would you use your problem-solving skills to overcome these challenges and win?

- use large marshmallows
- try the problem blindfolded
- build outside on a windy day
- make a rule that your tower has to be over a certain height
- set the timer for 3 minutes

GHOSTBUSTER LOOP

_ □ X

In coding, a **loop** is something programmers may use if they want the computer to repeat a specific action until a **condition** is met. Loops are used so the same instruction does not have to be written every time the code requires it. Loops save time and space by putting the command on repeat. In this activity, you will follow the loops to destroy some ghosts!

YOU WILL NEED: _ □ X

- a die
- coins
- a small object to move around on the grid
- a timer set for 5 minutes
- a sharp eye!

You are a famous ghost hunter. You have been called in to rid a haunted house of its pesky ghosts. Use the grid boxes and the chart to guide you.

LET'S FOLLOW THE LOOPS!

First, place your object on any empty square on the grid. Then, follow the loops on the chart according to what is true or false for the box you land on in the grid. Try to take all the ghosts out of the house in 5 minutes or less! Once you have blasted a ghost, cover it with a coin to show it has been zapped!

START THE TIMER

↓

Roll the die. Move your game piece that many squares in any direction through the haunted house.

 LOOP

LOOP

↓

Use ghost spray to blast it away! ← **TRUE** ← The square has a ghost. → **FALSE** → No ghost here! Keep searching!

TURN THE PAGE TO BUST MORE GHOSTS!

How did you do? Were you able to follow the loops in the program? How many ghosts did you destroy? Can you think of a way to make the job easier? What would you do differently?

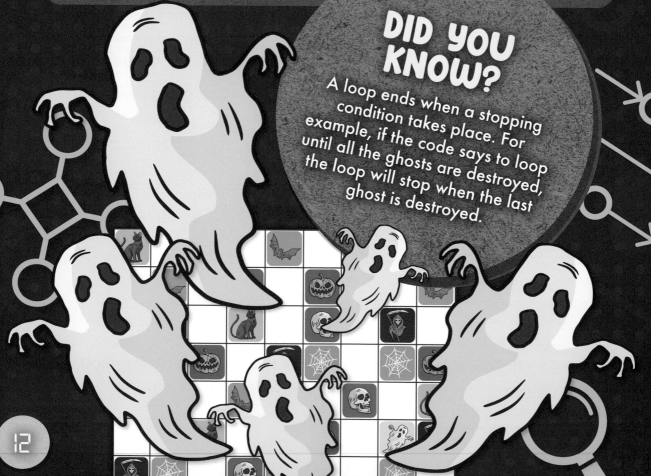

DID YOU KNOW?

A loop ends when a stopping condition takes place. For example, if the code says to loop until all the ghosts are destroyed, the loop will stop when the last ghost is destroyed.

CODING CHALLENGE! _ □ X

One person is the ghost hunter, and the other person is the coder.

You Will Need:
- a friend
- an outdoor paved area
- sidewalk chalk
- a timer

1. On a flat paved area, use sidewalk chalk to create a 6x6 grid with six rows of six equal-sized squares.
2. Draw ghosts in any five squares.
3. Mark a green dot in a different square for the start.
4. The ghost hunter stands on the green dot, holding a piece of chalk.
5. The coder starts the timer for 3 minutes. The coder gives commands such as "walk three steps" or "turn right" to the ghost hunter.
Each time the ghost hunter enters a square that has a ghost, the ghost hunter draws an X on it. That removes the ghost from the haunted house. The coder tries to get the ghost hunter to every square with a ghost before the time runs out!

AN ALIEN SPACESHIP

_ □ **X**

Have you ever had to take apart something to see if you could fix it? Solving a problem by looking at each of the separate parts is what programmers call decomposition. By breaking down a code into small chunks, programmers make it easier to find errors if something goes wrong. They can then **debug** those errors. They can also copy the chunks of code into other programs.

Your challenge is to use decomposition to design a spaceship for an alien. How will you break down the problem to help the alien land safely?

YOU WILL NEED: _ □ X

- an outdoor space
- an egg
- markers
- craft supplies such as glue and tape
- newspaper
- straws
- plastic wrap
- balloons
- rubber bands
- popsicle sticks
- a blanket
- feathers
- cotton balls
- a container to be the frame for the spaceship

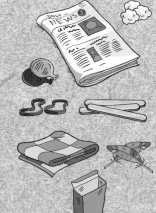

LET'S GIVE DECOMPOSITION A TRY!

14

1 Use an egg to represent the alien. Use markers to add features to your alien-egg.

2 Think about the materials you will use to build the spaceship and the way you will build it. You must be able to drop the spaceship from high above the ground without breaking the alien-egg inside.

3 Use the materials to build your alien's spaceship, creating a spot to hold the alien-egg.

4 When you have built your spaceship, place the alien-egg inside it.

5 Stand on a sturdy chair or outdoor staircase and drop the spaceship. You will know your decomposition skills were successful if the alien-egg is unbroken after landing!

DID YOU KNOW?

Coders follow a series of steps when using decomposition. First, they start with understanding what the problem or task is. Then, they break it into smaller steps. Finally, they write the code and test it.

TURN THE PAGE TO REVIEW HOW YOU DID!

15

CHECK IT OUT!

How did you use decomposition to break down the problem into steps? Did your alien-egg have a safe landing? What steps did you find challenging? Did your design work the way you expected?
What would you change if you did it again?

HERE'S A TIP!

Think like a programmer! When you have a problem to decompose, work backward. Know the end goal, and then plan the steps you must take to achieve it.

CODING CHALLENGE!

— ▢ X

Play this game with several friends. Your crew must work together to help a UFO land safely. Use a hula hoop as the UFO. Ask your friends to stand in a circle and hold out their arms with their pointer fingers out, fingerprint side up. Ask an adult to place the hoop on the fingers so that it rests on them. Each person must keep their fingertips in contact with the hula hoop at all times. The hoop should balance on the tips of their fingers. No one may hook their fingers around the hoop or hold it in any way. The challenge is to lower the hoop to the ground without dropping it. Can you and your friends decompose the problem to land the UFO safely?

SCARY SCENT!

_ □ X

In coding, a **variable** is a way of holding information known as **values** within the code. Just like a haunted house can have different ghosts, each variable can store values that can change. There are different types of variables for different purposes.

YOU WILL NEED: _ □ X

- a variety of colored beads
- yarn or string
- paper
- a pencil

Take a look at variables and values with this activity to scare off vampires. Some people believe that wearing a string of garlic bulbs will keep vampires away. To make this activity less smelly, we will make bead bracelets! You will use your bracelet as a variable to hold values of beads. This will help you create a code for scaring off vampires!

I'M NOT SCARED!

1

Choose six different-colored beads. Set a value for each bead by assigning a letter in the word "garlic" to each color. For example, a blue bead may represent the letter "g," and a yellow one could stand for "a." Write down the colors and their values.

DID YOU KNOW?

By writing down variables and their values, you are creating a way to remember, or store, information. When a code includes variables, the computer uses them to store the information.

2

String the beads on the yarn in the correct order to complete the word "garlic."

3

Loop 3 times to increase the number of times "garlic" is repeated. Now you are really protected!

4

Wear your garlic bracelet to scare away vampires!

TURN THE PAGE FOR MORE BEADING FUN!

19

How did your bead bracelet turn out? Were you able to give each colored bead its own letter value to spell the word? What effect does looping the word "garlic" have on your protection from vampires?

HERE'S A TIP!

Think about how your brain stores information in its memory. A computer stores information in its memory, too. Each variable must be given its own name so the computer can remember it and use the values correctly.

CODING CHALLENGE! _ □ X

Make another bracelet or a necklace. Think of other ways to give values to the beads. Values can be letters, numbers, or even words. Can you think of a way to make it work? How would you design it? Perhaps your message will fill an entire necklace!

I HOPE YOU ENJOYED UNPLUGGED CODING!

GLOSSARY

code—instructions for a computer

commands—specific instructions to complete a task

communicate—to share knowledge or information

condition—something that must occur before another action takes place

debug—to find and remove mistakes in code

decomposition—the process of breaking down a problem or system into smaller parts

loop—a group of code that can be easily repeated

paranormal—unusual events that cannot be explained by science

UFOs—unidentified flying objects; UFOs are often thought to be alien spacecraft, although any unknown flying object can be called a UFO.

values—pieces of information in a code; values are often part of a variable.

variable—part of a code that stores information; variables contain related values.

TO LEARN MORE

AT THE LIBRARY

Cauduro, Monica Oriani. *Coding for Kids 3: Create Your Own App with App Inventor.* New York, N.Y.: White Star Publishers, 2020.

McCue, Camille. *Getting Started with Coding: Get Creative with Code!* Indianapolis, Ind.: John Wiley and Sons, 2019.

Prottsman, Kiki. *How to Be a Coder.* New York, N.Y.: DK Publishing, 2019.

ON THE WEB

FACTSURFER

Factsurfer.com gives you a safe, fun way to find more information.

1. Go to www.factsurfer.com.

2. Enter "coding with the paranormal" into the search box and click 🔍.

3. Select your book cover to see a list of related content.

INDEX